THE FACTS ON
NEAR-DEATH
EXPERIENCES

John Ankerberg
& John Weldon

HARVEST HOUSE PUBLISHERS
Eugene, Oregon 97402

Cover by Terry Dugan Design, Minneapolis, Minnesota.

Other books by
John Ankerberg & John Weldon

THE FACTS ON NEAR-DEATH EXPERIENCES

Copyright © 1996 by the Ankerberg Theological Research Institute
Published by Harvest House Publishers
Eugene, Oregon 97402

ISBN 1-56507-455-6

Printed in the United States of America.

97   98   99   00   01   02   /   LP   /   9   8   7   6   5   4   3   2

CONTENTS

A Personal Message

"The suspense is killing me..."

"There's no point to remaining in this world when heaven is just a step away..."

"I'm sorry, but don't be sad for me, please be joyous— I am about to enter the next life..."

—excerpts from suicide notes

The following story of Allison (Alli) Bierma was written by her parents, Bob and Debbie Bierma, and Pastor Manny Martinez. The story was also read for accuracy and approval by Reverend Keita Andrews, one of the men who found Alli's body. We decided to begin our booklet this way because it underscores our conviction, documented herein, that the "heavenly" near-death experience has more negative implications for American society than most people suspect. One of these consequences is, given the right conditions, an inducement to suicide:

Alli's Story

It was Sunday, June 5, 1994. We had just arrived home from church when the police officers came to the front door and gave us the news that would change our lives forever, "A female body has been found at the bottom of a cliff in Rocky Mountain National Park. As yet it hasn't been identified."

There had been an intense, statewide search, and the body they discovered was surely that of our daughter Alli. It had been seventeen days since she disappeared following the death of her boyfriend who had committed suicide a few days earlier. Now it seemed that our last thread of hope was gone.

Alli was a beautiful 18-year-old who loved to hike in the mountains. She was co-most valuable player on the high school volleyball team that placed fourth in the state. Being highly motivated and a straight A student, she was anxious to enroll at the University of Colorado in the fall.

As a child, Alli was obedient, happy, and fun loving with

a great smile. She had lots of friends and was involved in a variety of activities. As she grew older, the youth group at church began to play an important role in her life, and it was there that she trusted Christ as her Savior. Her faith was very important to her, and she lived her life accordingly.

It was also at this youth group that Alli began dating a boy, and they started sharing dreams of a future together for Christ. In fact, his desire to become a minister led him to share his faith at his high school before the whole student body. During his senior year he went to Germany as a foreign exchange student and lived at the home of a minister and his family. What a blessing we all thought this was going to be.

Tragically, the minister in Germany believed that the Bible taught that it was okay to engage in pornography and sexual promiscuity and ridiculed Alli's boyfriend for his convictions. This new life-style he was witnessing was contrary to the Christian beliefs he had always held. At this point, he began questioning his own faith. This confusion—and the fact that he missed Alli very much—prompted him to come home three months early. Upon his return, we sensed an uneasiness about him.

The following year when he went off to college, he studied philosophy and began a quest for answers to life. He read books on Hinduism and Buddhism and started experimenting with drugs. On one occasion, after he took LSD and had a "bad trip," he was hospitalized for 72 hours. Nevertheless, he continued using drugs and went into a deep depression.

Alli remained loyal to him throughout his personal turmoil, clinging to the dream of their marriage which included his becoming a minister and her becoming a Christian counselor. She thought of him as her first patient. They would debate for hours. She tried to bring him back to where he was before all this, but he asked her questions that she was not prepared to answer biblically, and he eventually took his own life.

She had tried hard to find answers to his problems as she read books like *Mere Christianity* by C.S. Lewis and *Peace with God* by Billy Graham, but she also looked for answers outside Christian writings and the Bible. Unfortunately, she read *Embraced by the Light,* by Betty Eadie, which is the story of the author's "death" and the deal she made with "Jesus Christ" to return to earth. This proved to be literally fatal for Alli because it gave her false ideas about dying.

On the day of her boyfriend's death, Alli went to her room and, with Eadie's book open on her desk, she began writing his eulogy and her own suicide note. Apparently, after examining *Embraced by the Light,* Alli reasoned that if she died she could join her boyfriend in heaven. Furthermore, she assumed from reading Eadie's book that death would not necessarily be final, but merely a transitional stage, and if God wanted her to, she would return to life.

As the next few days went by, Alli continued writing her suicide note. On the second day after her boyfriend's funeral, she drove to the mountains she loved, climbed a cliff, and took her own life. Seventeen days later, after hundreds of professional searchers gave up looking for her, two dedicated Christian men were led through providential circumstances directly to her body. An eight-page suicide note was found in her back pocket. While reading the note with a pastor friend, we became aware of a definite theme. The book *Embraced by the Light* gave Alli unbiblical thoughts about life and death—

> If God still wants me on this earth, I will not leave. If and when I leave it will be meant to be. And I will be more than willing to return if God asks me to.

> We must have planned to come to this world together and be a family a *long* time ago....I could not have asked for better parents on this earth....I feel my greatest lesson on earth has already been learned...to love unconditionally....More lessons on earth could have been learned but I will always continue to grow no matter where I am.

> Please pray that I may have assistance on the other side....I will be watching over you until you come home....Death is not so bad...death and birth have become a part of each other.

Now that Alli is gone, she will not be returning as *Embraced by the Light* deceptively suggested to her. Our prayer is that other young people during their time of pain, will not fall prey to false doctrines as Alli did. It is important that young people learn to study the Word of God. If Alli had understood one biblical principle, she would still be alive today. That principle is: God will *never* lead someone to do something that is contrary to His Word.

In Alli's eight-page suicide letter there were no less than 14 points of similarity to ideas related in the popular near-death experience (NDE) literature. As we show in Question 2, those who argue NDEs do not precipitate suicide are wrong. However, as tragic as suicide is, the issue of the NDE for society involves far larger ramifications.

Section I

The Hidden Consequences of the Near-Death Experience (NDE)

Death cancels everything but truth.

—Anonymous

1. Why are NDEs a more vital subject than people think?

Most of us are familiar with the common elements of the popularly reported composite near-death experience. After undergoing a near-fatal car accident, heart attack, or other physical tragedy, a person is near death or declared "clinically dead." He or she has the perception of being "out of the body," looking down at his or her body while resuscitation attempts are made. The person soon finds they are in another location (or dimension) where the spirit world is encountered. This world is perceived as one of utterly indescribable love, beauty, peace, joy, and contentment. The individual may engage in telepathic or verbal communication with various spirits—usually of dead friends and relatives or a being (or beings) of light. Various teachings may be communicated and there may be a "review" of the person's life. Eventually the person finds himself approaching a barrier or border that he or she is not allowed to cross. The individual is instructed to return to his body because the time for him to die has not yet arrive.

The exact number of people who have had NDEs is not known, but estimates range from 2 to 20 million. No one can deny that through TV and radio interviews, discussions, newspaper articles, and books on the topic, tens and perhaps hundreds of millions of people worldwide have been exposed to the popularly interpreted message of the NDEs—that there is nothing to fear in death and that a heavenly glory awaits us all.

But there is also a negative side to NDEs that paints a far different picture than the rosy portrait commonly described. Also, as we will see in Question 7, the manner in which NDEs are researched and reported bears critical examination.

But let's start with the social impact. In evaluating the NDE critically, we should be concerned with more than just the possible negative effects upon people who have experienced NDEs themselves. Directly or indirectly, how this phenomenon is perceived has the potential to dramatically affect society on views of both death *and* life. How a society views death significantly influences how it views life and, as some researchers argue, the NDE "seems to have changed permanently our understanding of death" (39:xiii).

According to prominent NDE researcher Kenneth Ring of the University of Connecticut, NDEs even affect those who never have them: "We now know, from the latest research on NDEs, that even persons who are exposed to the literature on NDEs and come to take an interest in it, also *begin to experience changes in their lives akin to those that near-death experiencers report*....Furthermore, in one study, it has been shown that more than 80 percent of such persons state that their own fear of death has diminished..." (39:xiii).

Dr. Cherie Sutherland concludes her published dissertation research on NDEs by claiming the "potential force for positive social changes is enormous" and that the NDEs presage "a profound transformation of great benefit to society as a whole"(3:243). But it depends on one's perspective. Certainly NDEs, as commonly perceived, will continue to affect society. But how and in which direction?

In *The Light Beyond*, Raymond Moody, M.D., the first researcher to publish a landmark bestseller on NDEs, points out how surprised he was at the longevity of interest in the NDE. He recalls that, in 20 years, no matter where he has gone worldwide, people are fascinated by the subject because they want answers to the meaning of death and life (2:78-81). In fact, this really isn't surprising; it underscores the common human interest in issues of great personal significance. People want meaning to their lives, and if

NDEs—even NDEs experienced by others—seem to provide such meaning, people will want to know more.

Dr. Douglas Groothuis comments, "Unless we find some meaning to death, we will see no meaning to life, for our lives are permeated by death" (15:10). Indeed, perhaps the seminal work on the subject of death is the Pulitzer prize-winning book, *The Denial of Death* by cultural anthropologist Ernest Becker. Becker shows that death saturates our lives and yet remains a subject avoided at almost every level of our existence. Whether consciously or not we ignore, silence, camouflage, isolate and deny death: (16)

> The prospect of death, Dr. Johnson said, wonderfully concentrates the mind. The main thesis of this book is that it does much more than that. The idea of death, the fear of it, haunts the human animal like nothing else....the fear of death is indeed a universal in the human condition....of all things that move man, one of the principal ones is his terror of death...(40:ix,ii).

As Socrates stated in Plato's *Apology,* "Nobody knows, in fact, what death is, nor whether to man it is not per chance the greatest of blessings; yet people fear it as if they surely knew it to be the worst of evils."

So how do we begin to evaluate the near-death experience? There is absolutely no doubt that the NDE is *perceived* as a real experience. The key issue, then, is properly interpreting the experiences people perceive. For example, despite widespread popular belief, the NDE is *not* an experience of true death, as researchers concede, nor is it unique. In actual fact, it "has nothing inherently to do with death or with the transition to death" (5:226). And, as many have pointed out, those who have mystical experiences entirely apart from death "are just as transformed as those who have a near-death experience" (4:172/14:23-25/1:113). Placed in its proper context, the NDE is simply one of a larger number of mystical experiences, most of which have similar results. So while the NDE is real, it is not associated with death per se, nor is it unique in terms of its aftereffects. But are NDE aftereffects really what they seem to be?

Raymond Moody claims that a common belief among most NDE researchers is that the results of the NDE are entirely positive:

There is one common element in all near-death experiences: they transform the people who have them. In my twenty years of intense exposure to NDErs, I have yet to find one who hasn't had a very deep and *positive* transformation as a result of his experience....All the scholars and clinicians I have talked to who have interviewed NDErs come to the same conclusion: they are *better people* because of their experience" (2:33-34e).

People are certainly changed. But again, "for the better" depends on one's perspective. All NDE researchers agree that dramatic alterations in personality, worldview, relationships, and so on, can result from NDEs. In many cases, NDEs "tend to confer a new personal identity upon the NDEr as well as bring about major changes in behavior" (5:120). As three NDErs have remarked: "It's like one life ended, one life began"; "After the first death, I returned to a body with the same name, but little else in common with the woman who had died. Many of my memories were wiped out. What remained or returned seemed more like a movie"; "I truly feel as if the old me really did die and the new me has difficulty remembering what went on before" (1:78-79).

Despite its widespread, popular image as a heavenly experience, we will catalog some of the *negative* effects of NDEs. First, there is an estimated 10 to 50 percent of often thoroughly *hellish* NDEs, (15:69-87/17:105-14/18:27-45/14:28). But there are other potentially troubling consequences from the experiences themselves and how they have been interpreted in our culture. The next two questions reveal that, far from being a life-affirming experience, NDEs can have association with a more permanent death.

2. Do NDEs decrease or increase suicidal tendencies?

Most NDE researchers claim that the near-death experience does not encourage people to commit suicide merely to experience the indescribable glories of the afterlife. The reason researchers usually give is twofold: 1) individuals who commit suicide and then have an NDE seem to come back with the conviction that their suicide attempt was not a solution to their problems, and 2) some people have it communicated to them during their NDE that suicide is a "sin."

If a final loss of hope is a primary reason for suicide, it could be expected that the intensely meaningful nature of the NDE would, at least temporarily, alleviate the problem. Life may be considered much less of a burden if people believe that heaven is guaranteed at death.

We still believe the NDE can lead to suicide—and may do so in more cases than we are led to believe. First, the social climate surrounding death is far more liberal than a generation ago. There is not only an increasing acceptance of euthanasia but, in some quarters, a move toward the acceptance of suicide as a person's right, regardless of the reasons given. Second, the NDE message communicated to many is that "God" or the "being of light" is entirely nonjudgmental; therefore, there are no *final* or ultimate consequences even for suicide. Third, NDE researchers who argue that suicide should not be considered because it prevents "opportunities for growth" generally mean that it prevents opportunities for growth in this life. Thus, if life is too miserable for a person, and there are no penalties for suicide in the next life—indeed, only endless *opportunities* for growth—then, given the blissful portrayal of the NDE, on what logical basis would a despondent person *not* consider suicide? Couldn't one assume it would be much more preferable to kill oneself if it gets rid of the pain and leads to residing forever in heaven? At the very least, a person might consider to no longer continue to live in the torment of this life over which they have no seeming control.

People magazine, in their November 11, 1995, issue, reported the suicide of two love-struck teenagers, ages 13 and 14, who killed themselves so they could be together in the afterlife. The 13-year-old girl wrote to her parents concerning her boyfriend, "Mom and Dad...you won't let me see him in this world, so we're going to another place."

Alli Bierma, the young girl whose story we shared earlier, wrote the following in her own suicide note:

> I'm in pain here....Soon I will be home at last with him [Alli's boyfriend] and most of all my Heavenly Father. Oh, how I have been longing for the day! What great joy it brings me to think of home! Some people in this world are strong enough to run through to the finish line. I, however, have decided to bring the finish line to me instead of gasping for air. I'm tired and I want to go home....I feel that my greatest lesson on earth has already been learned.

To love unconditionally. Love is the meaning of this life I believe. I understand there would have been more lessons to grow from but I will always continue to grow no matter where I am....I merely want to go home now and hope everyone will understand why. Much is waiting for me and I long to be in God's arms.

According to *The Denver Post,* June 6, 1994, Alli "had told friend Bill Matlock that her boyfriend's suicide angered her immensely and she vowed she would never put anyone through such pain." So what would have influenced Alli's suicide if *not* Eadie's *Embraced by the Light*? Even Pastor Manny Martinez, a close friend of the family said, "This book is greatly responsible for what happened to Alli" (open letter, June 1994). And Eadie's own statement does not discourage suicide in light of other statements in her book. She said, "We must never consider suicide. This act will only cause us to lose opportunities for further development while here on earth" (20:70). Wasn't Alli's response in conformity with other teachings or the book: "I feel my greatest lesson on earth has already been learned"? And didn't Eadie also teach, "Our deaths are also often calculated to help us grow.....Some people choose to die in ways that will help someone else" (20:67-68)? Indeed, there are at least a dozen strong points of similarity between Eadie's *Embraced by the Light* and Alli's suicide note. To say Eadie's book had *no* influence on Alli's decision to commit suicide is false.

Further, those NDErs who believe it was communicated to them that suicide is wrong, seem to feel it's wrong only for them, but that it could be right for others. One NDEr, who had previously considered suicide because of intense pain stated, "The one thing I got when I was up there was that I would never get back there by committing suicide, and that my task was to serve. But that was for me personally, it wasn't a general statement for every person. There are some people I know who've committed suicide. It's a path for some people. It's just not my path..."(3:86-87).

In fact, NDEs may increase the acceptance of suicide among NDErs simply because they "know" the person will be better off: "Janet, who was adamant she would never commit suicide herself, said: 'I feel that if a person did commit suicide, they would be met with total love and compassion, as I was. God is just total love'" (3:87). Dr.

Cherie Sutherland concluded, "The NDE seems to cause a definite shift in attitude when it comes to the suicide of others. Although strongly against suicide for themselves, several of the near-death experiencers felt compassion and sadness for those who do commit suicide. They claim they have learned from their own NDE that there is no point in suicide, but realize that, as Shana said: 'it's a path for some.' Eight people suggested suicide was a matter for the individual to decide, whereas *none* claimed to have thought this *before* their NDE" (3:87e).

Some NDEs per se encourage suicide. In *Closer to the Light: Learning from the Near-Death Experiences of Children*, Dr. Morse reveals that a 14-year-old boy who described his experience several years later commented that the Light, "solicited death as a means to a different and better life" (19:137). In another case, a 10-year-old saw a vast "sea of light." "I was urged to jump into it....No voice said this: it just came to me from a kind of presence....In an instant, I knew...I'd never...get back home" (19:163).

While preliminary research indicates that people who have NDEs do not take their own lives in order to go back into the light, we think it is too early to generalize. As noted, with suicide attempts, the NDE could be expected to bring a renewed sense of purpose and importance to life that would counter the negative experiences that caused people to attempt suicide. On the other hand, what if their life deteriorates to the previous condition? What if a person's life becomes unbearable? Compounding the issue for many NDErs, the NDE *causes* serious problems in life. All this suggests there is no guarantee NDErs will not commit suicide to go back into "the light." Even NDE researcher P.M.H. Atwater refers to, "a lessening of the desire to live" and "a temptation to return to 'The Other Side.' Any struggle to live can appear meaningless or unnecessary. *It would be so easy to go back*. This temptation can linger, even for *years*, slowing full recovery" (1:102e).

Raymond Moody agrees that NDErs "almost long for the blissful state of existence that they discovered in their NDE" (2:52). And, he asks, "Why shouldn't NDErs have difficulty readjusting? Once you've experienced a spiritual paradise, wouldn't returning to the world be a drag for anyone?" (2:50). Again, Atwater remarks, "How are you going to return to what now seems petty comings and goings once you have experienced a perfect world and a greater reality? Can you imagine what it would be like to suddenly find yourself in another dimension or world where, like some kind of god, you had all knowledge, all peace, all love, all light, all freedom, all joy?...You never forget it. You can't. It leaves a mark too deep and profound....[F]ormer stereotypes and traditions, rules and prejudices, goals and achievements are challenged, or become like so much garbage" (1:92-93).

As one NDEr says, "I really didn't have much desire to go on living. I really wanted to go back...I really wanted to die" (5:93).

Not surprisingly then, "The vast majority feel more as if they have been resentenced to *prison*, for that shell of their former residence now feels somehow small, tight, confining, uncomfortable, clumsy, unnatural. They feel alienated—from the very body that had nourished the formation of their personal identity since birth. They now know *they are not their body*! They feel boxed in....[As one said] 'My body is something I put up with. It's the baggage I carry on my trip through life...'" (1:99e).

In *Embraced by the Light*, which TV ads claim sold some 6 million copies its first two years, committed Mormon Betty Eadie recalls her adamant refusal to return to the horrible conditions of this life. (Despite dedicating the book to "My Lord and Savior Jesus Christ" her NDE reflects Mormon theology throughout, not biblical teaching.) When, during the NDE, she was told by her spirit guides she must return to complete her "mission" on earth, she recalled, "Without hesitation, I said, 'No, no. I can't go back. I belong here. This is my home.' I stood firm, knowing that nothing could ever make me choose to leave....I was *not* going back....I threw myself down and began crying. 'I *won't* go back,' I wailed, 'And nobody is going to make me! I'm staying right here where I belong. I'm *through* with earth!'" (20:117-18). Finally persuaded to return, as she reentered her body it was a truly horrible experience,

> I stood in the air and looked down at it and was filled with *revulsion*. It looked cold and heavy and reminded me of an old pair of coveralls that had been dragged through *mud and grime*. In comparison, I felt like I had just taken a long, soothing shower, and now I had to put that *heavy, cold, muddy* garment on....The body's cumbersome weight and coldness were *abhorrent*....I became inconsolably *depressed*. After the joy of spiritual freedom, I had become a

prisoner to the *flesh* again. As I lay *trapped* in the body, my three ancient friends [spirit guides] appeared at my bed again. My dear monks, my ministering spirits, had come to comfort me (20:123-24e).

Such perceptions are hardly unique among NDErs. So isn't it possible that NDErs who have known "heaven" but now live back where they were might find it just a bit difficult to continue their "torment"? If earthly life is, at best, a spiritual constraint that death releases us from, what is the real message conveyed? In *Transformed by the Light,* Melvin Morse, M.D., writes that the NDE has "profound implications for those of us who work with death and dying" and also for the "right to die" movement (4:220,232). Indeed. But what seems to be lost upon some researchers is that by their very nature, most NDEs cause a *loss* of the fear of death. But isn't the fear of death precisely what keeps most people from committing suicide? Dr. Morse agrees it should be recognized "that near-death experiences may make death more attractive to those considering suicide" (4:236).

Remember that Alli gave as the reason for her committing suicide her longing to go home to be with her "Heavenly Father." Her very argument was that even though she could have learned additional lessons on earth, she would continue to grow regardless of where she was. In fact, she rationalized that if it was *not* her "time" to go, the suicide would not end her life and she would, like so many other NDErs, be forced to "go back." Part of the reason suicide was attractive to her was because her boyfriend had committed suicide and she longed to be with him. One can only wonder how many other impressionable teenagers (or adults) have similar longings that NDEs and their popular interpretation could galvanize into desperate actions? It is well known that suicide is now a leading cause of death among teenagers.

As Doug Groothuis points out, far more than the NDE, it is the biblical view of life and death that inhibits suicide. People who feel they are responsible to God in this life are much less likely to commit suicide than those who believe that no one holds them accountable after death. The biblical teaching of eternal hell is also a strong restraint. Who would ever kill themselves if they thought they might *really* go to hell? But the "positive" NDE experience powerfully relays the message there is no hell for anyone—that all people will enter into a glorious and eternal paradise. Death is the friend to all and the enemy to none.

In light of the above, we believe that the NDE and its perception in our culture is more likely to increase suicide than decrease it.

3. What about abortion and NDEs?

Because all human life is unique and precious, abortion has become the single worst tragedy in our nation's history, with over *30 million* people dead who would otherwise be living. (See our booklet *The Facts on Abortion* for further study.) Jesus once called the devil "the father of lies" and "a murderer from the beginning" (John 8:44). As an evil being, what Satan desires is people's destruction. Obviously, abortion and suicide are good contenders for Satan's use. Yet, biblically forbidden practices such as channeling and mediumistic contact with the alleged dead (Deuteronomy 18:10-12), as well as the modern NDE, may justify abortion. In *Emmanuel's Book,* by channeler Pat Rodegast, the spirit calling itself "Emmanuel" says that abortion is "a useful act" when done "with willingness to learn" for "nothing in your human world is absolutely wrong" (21:201). Abortion is condoned because the "dead body" is considered far less important than the spirit that inhabits and animates it later. And the spirit has already possessed innumerable bodies throughout its reincarnation history so one more body is almost irrelevant.

Those who listen to messages communicated through more traditional mediums say the same thing: "As the soul of the baby whom this woman aborted attests, he is still alive; only his body died. Time and again [medium] George [Anderson] has received the same [spirit] message from children lost to abortion." In answering the question, What do the souls of children who have been aborted reveal to him? Anderson responds, "Often the soul that would have entered the body right before birth—which is the time they [the dead] tell me that occurs—will come through [me as a channel]....if there is a heavy sense of guilt attached to the abortion, the soul will put them [the mothers] at peace by saying, 'I might not have liked the idea of you stopping the process, but I understand why you did it.' I have had souls come through and say that they will come back again when it is a better time. Or that they left the body because they could see that there was a problem, physically....[Souls of aborted children] nearly always reassure their parents that they are at peace where they are. They never say that they were murdered....I've never had the soul that would have entered the body of an aborted fetus come through and say anything other than that they understood" (22:296, 302).

But among NDErs we find similar teachings: "[NDErs] speak of the soul's entry into the physical body around the time of birth and at death the soul simply leaves the body and goes on with its travels" (1:98). One NDEr, who had her abortion at 10 weeks, met her aborted baby in the spirit world, now an adult. He told her not to worry, that he wasn't even in the body when she had her abortion and that (contrary to medical evidence) there was no pain experienced in the procedure. As "Emmanuel" teaches, "[W]hen a soul chooses to be born, it will be born. The soul is wise and would not inhabit a body if it were not to come to term....Should one feel guilt? No..." (21:201).

In her phenomenal bestseller *Embraced by the Light,* Eadie says, "I learned that spirits can choose to enter their mother's body at any stage of her pregnancy." Even though abortion is said to be "unnatural," the spirit coming to the body "feels compassion for its mother, knowing that she had made a decision [for abortion] based on the knowledge she had" (20:95). Eadie's executive assistant, Tom Brittan, said that Eadie believes that abortion is "not sin at all" and that aborted bodies do not even have a spirit (43:41).

4. What are some theological consequences of the NDE and its popular interpretation?

Sufficient research has not been done to declare that the "average" NDE always conveys a specific religious or philosophical message. If current NDE research is metaphysically biased (see Question 7) then certain deficiencies exist in the common interpretation of NDEs. However, this is hardly to say that the common interpretation is always wrong or rarely reflects what people experience, only that those who experience it may be fewer than supposed. Given this caveat, let's proceed to a brief analysis of the implications of the NDE as commonly communicated. NDE researchers would probably agree with NDEr and NDE researcher P.M.H. Atwater when she writes, "Most [NDErs] fall head over heels in love with God....they were bathed in God, immersed in God, filled to overflowing with God; and they return convinced of God....They *know* God is" (1:109).

Unfortunately, in many cases the NDE experience itself and the message(s) conveyed turn people *away* from God, as well as Jesus Christ, Christian doctrines, and the Bible. (In the following accounts, use of the term "Christian" may be considered suspect if the researchers have not been careful to define it accurately.)

Moody points out that although most NDErs become spiritual they do not enter the church but instead come to reject its doctrines. Indeed, "they tend to abandon religious doctrine purely for the sake of doctrine" (2:49). In fact, whether or not a person was religious or nonreligious prior to his NDE, "Both groups emerge with an appreciation of religion that is different from the narrowly defined one established by most churches. They come to realize through this experience that religion is not a matter of one 'right' group versus several 'wrong' groups. People who undergo an NDE come out of it saying that religion concerns your ability to love—not doctrines and denominations" (2:87). Biblically, of course, the acts of love are inseparable from true doctrine. If "God is love" (1 John 4:8), then to love God and what He has revealed in His word means to love with proper beliefs and actions, not mere sentimentalism (see 1 Corinthians 13:1-8; 1 John 3:16; 4:7-15)

But many NDEs convey a message that rejects this. As one NDEr commented, "A lot of people I know are going to be surprised when they find out that the Lord isn't interested in theology" (2:49). After her NDE, a devout and "doctrine-abiding Lutheran" concluded that God "didn't care about church doctrine at all" (2:88).

One child who had an NDE came to realize that "many elements of her near-death experience did not match with things she had been taught in Sunday school" (4:135). Atwater refers to the wife of a conservative Christian pastor who had an NDE:

> Since her experience, it has become increasingly difficult for her to attend her husband's church services: "He's wrong. I know now deep in my heart he's wrong. What he's preaching, that's not the way it is. I feel like he's telling everyone a lie and I don't know what to do about it. I love my husband and I love our children. I don't want to upset him or anyone else. I don't want a divorce or anything like that. But I can't listen anymore. I try to pretend I'm too busy to come" (1:110).

One committed Christian wrote that after her NDE, "I hold to the biblical interpretation of death. But having a firsthand experience like that has changed me in the way that I view possible [divine] judgment....I've come more to the view that judgment is something we do ourselves" (3:84).

A former member of the High Church of England wrote that before her NDE, "There was a lot of hellfire and damnation stuff. After the NDE, I rejected that....To me God is no longer a judgmental being....I don't attend a church [anymore] it's almost as though I feel I've got the answers" (3:99). Gary, brought up as a Baptist, became a Buddhist after his NDE: "I opened a copy of *Teachings of the Compassionate Buddha*, and it hit me like a 10-ton brick. I'm not joking....And here I was only 16, and never heard of Buddhism in my life" (3:100).

One pastor who preached on hell was told by the "being of light" "not to speak to his congregation like this anymore" (2:39).

Experiences that cause people to reject biblical truth can hardly be considered divine. Biblically, God *is* interested in doctrine because He is a God of truth. The Bible is full of God's commands that His people are to be earnestly concerned about "correct doctrine" (see 1 Timothy 6:3,4; Titus 1:9; Jude 3). And there *is* a final judgment (see Question 10).

The thirteenth "being of light" that instructed bestselling NDE author Dannion Brinkley (*Saved by the Light*) told him his purpose on earth was to "show people how to rely on their spiritual selves instead of the government and churches" (23:58).

Atwater reports,

> Traditional references to God such as Father, He, Him, or Mother, She, Her can become unacceptable....Preferred titles are ones such as The Force, The One, Universal Mind, The Source, All, The Divine—or just plain *God*....Of the survivors in my research...two-thirds either cast aside religious affiliations or were never involved to begin with. For these people, awareness most often shifts from standards and dogmas to what is commonly called "the spiritual quest."...Popular choices are metaphysical and "New Age" churches or Eastern systems. Those who prefer a more natural or simple approach usually gravitate to philosophies such as mysticism or practices such as shamanism. Regardless of religious

or spiritual preferences, the average near-death survivor is more interested in what is historically called "The Mysteries."...They are more in tune with gnosis...(1:110).

Indeed, we have already seen gnostic views of the body in Questions 2 and 3. Dr. Kenneth Ring comments on the essential agreement of the NDE and the ancient Egyptian Osirian rituals: "The NDE is, in its essence, identical to what the Osirian candidate learned during his initiation" (42:9).

Dr. Cherie Sutherland's study differentiated between people who were "religious" (part of organized religion) and "spiritual" (much broader in their religious outlook). The term "religious" was specifically connected with Christian churches, particular doctrines, and so on. She found the dominant shift was away from "religion" and towards "spirituality." Over 50 percent of her NDErs were affiliated with Protestant or Catholic churches before the NDE, but only 14 percent continued this after the NDE. For example, one person who, before the NDE "was quite religious," now declares she is "spiritual because I don't go to churches anymore. I don't belong to any denomination" (3:101). Michael, an NDEr, wrote, "Now I am more spiritual. I disagree with the church. I went for a while, one of my friends is a Christian....[The sermons I heard] were wrong as far as I was concerned" (3:102). Anthea stated that her views of organized religion changed after her NDE, "I felt less that they have the answers. I feel more that the answers come from within your own being" (3:104). Edwina observed, "I now have a very strong view that church and religion are totally divorced from spirituality. It doesn't matter what sort of religion you get involved with....I do believe in God but not in a traditional church God. I mean I believe that all that light [in the NDE] is what we call God" (3:104). Cora declared, "I have a feeling of anger and rage at the indoctrination of organized religion" (3:105). Helen said, "I feel that church is a bit of a sham" (3:106).

Sutherland's research concluded that there was "an established shift on all six [survey] items *away* from organized religion and church attendance and toward private nonformula prayer, meditation and a general quest for spiritual values" (3:104).

Although the vast majority of her study sample now claims to be *spiritual*, "eighty-four percent claim to have no religion, only six percent claim to be religious, eighty percent see no value in organized religion and 80 percent never attend church" (3:110).

Further, "Margo Grey found that 20 percent of her English NDErs shifted from orthodox Christianity to universalism after their NDEs, while an additional 27 percent converted to occult systems like spiritualism or Theosophy" (11:100).

Obviously, if we assume these accounts are valid, the thrust of these NDEs is clearly away from biblical doctrine, organized religion, church attendance, and so forth, to a more generalized New Age spirituality. Dr. Groothuis observes, "After their NDE, many have opted for a vague notion of God, spiritual knowledge without clear guidelines, and love without absolute moral demands" (15:91). In light of such information, we don't believe anyone can logically argue that NDEs are without significant theological implications. But there is more.

Of those who have a philosophy about life communicated to them during the NDE, most seem to experience one or more of three dominant perspectives: 1) a mediumistic view of the afterlife (see our *The Facts on Life After Death* for further study); 2) pantheistic beliefs; and 3) the "truth" of the concept of reincarnation, which we discuss in the next question. The problem is not only that each of these views supports the occult, but in its own way, each insulates one against a Christian and biblical worldview.

P.M.H. Atwater, a psychic and astrologer whom we briefly met at the 1988 American Federation of Astrologers Las Vegas Convention, claims three NDEs and that through them she realized "*God is all that is*" (1:145). Indeed, "I truly considered my winter coat to be a living, breathing friend of mine....I honestly could not distinguish between that which is living and that which is not. To me, everything breathed and everything was alive....To this day [11 years later], I still cannot always distinguish animate from inanimate" (1:76).

Another NDEr explained, "I was God, God was me" (1:69). In *Saved by the Light*, Dannion Brinkley was also told the "truth" of pantheism. The beings of light that instructed him to construct New Age centers for the dying said their major purpose was to show others how to regulate mystical energy in the body to help them recognize their own divinity. The spirits told him, "When you reach the point where you can control this energy and transform it into a positive force, you have found the part of you that is God" (23:161).

5. What about the NDEs that teach reincarnation?

The philosophy of reincarnation is also communicated in many NDEs. P.M.H. Atwater believes that "Reincarnation is a favorite topic for near-death survivors....For most, it becomes a fact of life" (1:141); and, "They talk about reincarnation as if it were an established fact and, almost to a person, mention a *life plan* and speak of how our lives follow rhythmic cycles of development" (1:100).

Dr. Sutherland's study indicated that "belief in reincarnation was also found to be noticeably strengthened" (3:41). In her doctoral research, approximately one-third of those who had NDEs already believed in reincarnation before their NDE, a figure close to that of the general [Australian] population. But after the NDE, more than *twice* as many believed in reincarnation. They offered such comments as, "I couldn't accept it at all, but I believe it absolutely now"; "Before I never gave it a thought but now I believe it definitely"; and, "I was aware of reincarnation, but didn't have the firm belief that I have now....now I definitely believe in reincarnation, I have no doubt about it at all" (3:84).

Polls indicate that about one in four Americans also believes in reincarnation. However, reincarnation is not only a false belief, it is an occult belief and one especially damaging to the gospel. The following material illustrates the arguments cited in favor of reincarnation and their problems. (Since reincarnation theories vary and even contradict one another, the following should be considered general.)

ARGUMENT 1
Reincarnation is taught in the Bible.

> *Response 1:* It can be demonstrated that no Scripture teaches reincarnation. One reason is because the God who inspired Scripture never contradicts Himself and the philosophical premises of reincarnation are antithetical to major biblical teachings: for example, self-perfection vs. salvation by grace apart from good works and individual merit; self-atonement (paying off one's own "karma") vs. Christ's atonement for *other's* sin. Indeed, if Christ paid the divine penalty for all sin ("karma") no "karma" remains to be worked

off individually. Regardless, "man is destined to die *once*, and after that to face judgment" (Hebrew 9:27 NIV).

Counter Response 1: Reincarnation was *originally* a teaching in the Bible but was deleted by church authorities due to theological bias.

Final Response 1: The orthodox and devout Jewish authors of the Bible would never have taught a *pagan* teaching that contradicted and denied their own beliefs and religion. This explains why no evidence—anywhere in church history—supports the fanciful notion of biblical expungement.

ARGUMENT 2
Since more and more karma is increasingly worked off along the path to perfection, reincarnation provides for an inevitable moral and spiritual progress for all humanity.

Response 2: All evidence suggests otherwise (reincarnation, according to the law of karma, is not working as it should).

Counter Response 2: Reincarnation provides the *opportunity* for progress, not the inevitability.

Final Response 2: It is still not working; mankind is morally unimproved historically. What suggests reincarnation will ever work, given its "millions" of years of impotence so far?

ARGUMENT 3
Reincarnation circumvents the nihilism of materialism.

Response 3: Each incarnation involves an entirely new person; each person's life is forever expunged at death, leading to the same nihilism of materialism. Every *individual* person exists only once in a meaningless *personal* life and is then extinguished for eternity. This offers similar consequences to materialism.

Counter Response 3: But there is individual life in *the soul* that reincarnates.

Final Response 3: It is still not the previous person and, in the end, is absorbed into the final impersonal reality regardless. In a universe where the individual person is a cipher and the Impersonal Divine the only infinite reference point and absolute reality, even the entire trajectory of the *personal* soul is finally meaningless.

ARGUMENT 4

Reincarnation offers a credible explanation for and resolution to the problem of evil.

> **Response 4:** Not only does it not explain the origin of evil, in theory it encourages and perpetuates evil eternally.

> **Counter Response 4:** Evil results from spiritual ignorance of our own divinity; universal realization of our inherent godhood will lead to the elimination of evil.

> **Final Response 4:** First, no evidence suggests man is one essence with God or part of God. Second, even the allegedly God-realized have never proven themselves sinless. Characteristically, they only redefine sin or evil as an illusion—which does nothing to end evil but tends to increase it. Third, reincarnation leads to even greater inequities, such as callousness toward the suffering of others, which must logically be interpreted as their karmic *justice* (the horrors of the caste system in India is illustrative). Fourth, most religious monistic systems ultimately reject absolute morality and imply that the "illusion" of evil exists forever. In Hinduism the divine soul is eternal; the final absorption of the individual soul in one cycle is only one of an infinite number of similar cycles. Practically speaking, evil, therefore, exists forever.

ARGUMENT 5

Because of the associated law of karma, reincarnation provides perfect justice.

> **Response 5:** *You* cease to exist at death; the person punished in the next life is not *you* but a new entity entirely. The fact that *it* is punished for *your* sins, is hardly "just."

> **Counter Response 5:** But *my* soul still lives on.

> **Final Response 5:** Again, it is not *your* soul, since *you* will not exist. Neither does it remember "its" sins to help it improve in the next life. Not only is this unjust, it is impractical. One cannot strive to improve

to a better standard without knowing the previous standard one failed to attain.

ARGUMENT 6
Reincarnation is a universal belief found in all cultures.

> *Response 6:* Most, but not all cultures. It is usually found among pagan and spiritually primitive cultures. They are pagan and primitive largely from the spiritual and other consequences of their religious philosophies, including reincarnation.

> **Counter Response 6:** That's just an opinion.

> *Final Response 6:* Given absolute moral standards and biblical teachings, such cultures are primitive morally and spiritually—by theological fact, not opinion. For example, in India one sees the real fruit of its spiritual philosophies.

ARGUMENT 7
Reincarnation allows the time needed for true self-perfection.

> *Response 7:* Actual self-perfection is impossible for a fallen race.

> *Counter Response 7:* Not over billions of years.

> *Final Response 7:* Neither the extent of human sinfulness nor the holiness of God is adequately comprehended. If the biblical view of human depravity is true, then in all eternity man could not perfect himself.

ARGUMENT 8
Reincarnation engenders personal responsibility.

> *Response 8:* As documented in occult writings and pagan history, it rationalizes or engenders amoralism, selfishness, immorality, and all sorts of evil—often justifying them by recourse to allegedly spiritual principles and truths.

> *Counter Response 8:* People are held accountable for what they do.

> *Final Response 8:* In reincarnation, people are not held accountable. *They* will never experience future judgment, either in the next life or any other life.

ARGUMENT 9

"Past life" experiences and therapy has proved reincarnation true.

> ***Response 9:*** "Past life" experiences, whether in therapy or outside it, are psychological or occult delusions. Such experiences do not help people, but harm them by seeming to justify a false and destructive philosophy or providing a false diagnosis and solution to people's problems.

> ***Counter Response 9:*** Therapists claim it has cured thousands of their patients.

> ***Final Response 9:*** Such therapists are violating their own tenets in seeking to counter the "justice" of karma. People who suffer from supposed past-life karma should be left to suffer. To seek to counteract karmic justice is a moral violation of the canons of reincarnation belief and will only result in additional karma. Presumably, the therapist will also reap his or her karma for the sin of interference.

For those who desire a more thorough biblical and critical evaluation of reincarnation, we suggest the books in reference 12.

6. What are the day-to-day consequences of many NDEs?

Although the dominant experience of the positive NDE includes an overwhelming sensation of love, one would hardly know it from some of the consequences of NDEs in many people's lives. If these experiences are divine, this is hardly what we would expect. On the other hand, if they are not divine, but spiritual counterfeits, this is just what we should expect. Below we survey some of these consequences.

People who have NDEs need understanding and sympathy because, for many, life becomes more difficult—sometimes even miserable. So many NDErs are having difficulties that researchers are now turning to an examination of this problem and looking for ways to help people with the psychological and other problems resulting from their NDE (3:80).

Based on her own negative experiences and those of the participants in her 1988 study, Atwater argues that NDErs get enraptured by the profundity of the experience, become disoriented and confused, wrapped up in themselves, and become, to varying degrees, unable to respond to the needs of others. She suggests that the love NDErs bring back is not love as commonly understood. Rather it is an impersonal detachment or sentimental emotionalism which can interfere with people's ability to personalize their feelings. The love these people mystically encounter, seemingly in harmony with the occult flavor of their NDE, is the kind of impersonal love spoken of in Eastern mystical experience (as in Hinduism and Buddhism). Atwater states: "The kind of love encounter[ed] in dying is not emotional....It is not personal....[It] is more...a transcended state of existence....This kind of love flows *through* you, not from or to you....This love, true love...makes no demand and seeks no response. It welcomes all and denies none....Existence in this kind of love *dissolves* all emotion, feelings, needs, and relationships" (1:70).

Atwater proceeds to explain that the allegedly unconditional and universal love "*can* cause more problems than it solves. It can hurt more than it helps....This kind of love can be more a nightmare than a blessing. It can drive a wedge between people. Let us be very practical about what unconditional love really means. *It means everyone is you and you are everyone*....It means you cannot divide or separate people, that you have no expectations, no needs, no wants, no conditions of any sort in loving. Love loses its object and becomes objectless" (1:72).

It's hardly surprising that a love that is impersonal; seeks no response; makes no demands; has no wants; welcomes all and denies none; dissolves all emotion, needs, and relationships; and becomes objectless, could produce some very difficult problems. Who can believe this is real love? As one NDEr reported, "The love my husband and I had shared flew out the window after I found universal love" (1:72). Another man emphasized, "I love my wife and children more than I ever thought I could. I love everyone. My experience taught me *real love, unconditional love!*" Nevertheless, "his wife and children did not feel the kind of love he described....he seemed somehow unreachable to them, as if he were 'floating' around somewhere in a world of his own, out of touch with the reality of what was really going on or what their personal needs were" (1:66).

As the above material hints, the NDE can also induce an undiscerning naivete and sentimentalism that leads to a variety of personal troubles and even disasters. Those who become uncritically accepting of others (and even the brutality of nature), who "love everything," and believe "God is all, all is love" often become victims of their own beliefs. Atwater herself confesses, "I am amazed at how many times survivors fall prey to repeated rapes, thefts, lies, cheating, losses of all kinds, fires, floods, financial setbacks, accidents, and to commitment to psychiatric treatment when none is really required. I myself was almost killed a number of times. We walk innocently into dangerous situations because we honestly do not recognize them as dangerous....We trust everyone because we know of no reason not to" (1:76).

For having been partakers of such a sublime and allegedly divine experience, NDErs seem to have encountered something a bit more nasty.

According to Dr. Sutherland's research, "Perhaps the most noticeable feature of the results is the major increase in the number of divorced people following the NDE....almost all ascribed their divorce *primarily* to the aftereffects of their NDE" (3:150-51). Dr. Morse reports, "Many times their spiritual transformation changes them so much that they become alienated from their families" (4:216).

One NDEr who describes why her marriage ended wrote, "I couldn't go back to the way I was. I was the proper mother, the proper wife, and active member of many, many community organizations....I wanted to be with dying people. I went back to school and became a respiratory therapist. And then, as this evolution of my own being became stronger and stronger, it did not fit into my own marriage anymore, so it had to end" (3:36).

Ironically, while many NDErs have a difficult time readjusting to life, at the same time they see themselves as uniquely blessed for having had such a special experience denied to others: "You are no longer like other people, and there's no use deceiving yourself that you are" (3:35). "Oftentimes, survivors become impatient and critical of others, feeling in some way better, and losing in that smugness the ability to understand the weakness and the fear people around them still deal with" (1:106). As one NDEr reported, "Relationships seem more intense, but only last a short time. I have no problems communicating but have found others cannot accept things as they are. I feel that everyone lives in a fantasy world, and I am the realist outcast" (1:106).

Problems of NDErs include not only trouble with relating to others but also difficulty with feeling that they belong to *anyone*, as well as an "inability to recognize and comprehend boundaries, rules or limits" (3:36). Further, "Previously familiar codes of conduct can lose some relevance or disappear altogether. The loss of boundaries, rules, and limits can take on many forms…" (1:75).

Some people accept this cosmic relativism while it obviously confuses others. Maurice Rawlings, M.D., mentions one incident where he had questioned a young man ready to donate plasma about the wounds on his body and the possibility of infecting others. Apparently guilt-ridden, the man then confessed he had murdered two individuals. He had also been shot by a transvestite after pummeling him for deceiving him into believing he was a woman. This man had undergone an NDE while being resuscitated in the ambulance. When Dr. Rawlings asked the man how he felt about it, he was somewhat perplexed, "Well, it felt good to be in this beautiful place, you know, but I kept wondering why the 'light' never asked me about my beating the heck out of this cross-dresser. And the light never mentioned the two killings in the past.…I knew I should be in hell instead of this nice place, but I kept quiet" (17:62). This person was aware he had committed terrible evil, but the implications of his NDE were unsettling. He asked, "Doc, does God ever make mistakes?"

If a murderer has a better sense of morality than the allegedly divine "light," then perhaps the "light" is not so divine after all. And if, after the NDE, "no longer can a person take refuge in the comfort of the conventional views and values of society," then what are the implications for us who live in society (3:39)?

Finally, most of the listed "categories of change" that occur in NDErs are interpreted as constituting positive results. But we may also question this. For example, in Sutherland's study under the chapter "Changes in Life Direction," she includes attitude to self, attitude to others, changes in relationships, attitude to life, lifestyle choices, and changes in interests. The positive changes include higher self-esteem and self-worth, an increase in self-understanding, less concern for other people's opinions, an increased desire for solitude, a greater sense of purpose, a desire to help others, more compassion and empathy, more expressions of love, and so on.

If self-esteem and self-worth are increased, in what *sense* are they increased, and how has this worked out practically in people's lives? Is it through prideful self-reliance upon one's inner "divine" nature or "higher self"— or through humble reliance upon the one true God? If one's self-understanding has increased, is this along the lines of biblical teaching or of humanistic, gnostic, and occult teaching?

What kind of "sense of purpose" do NDErs emerge with? Does this involve biblical concerns or does it involve New Age concerns such as being directed by "beings of light" or "angels" for *their* own purposes? Many NDErs come back with a "mission" to help people who are dying. They seem compelled to do so in order to help the dying realize there is no death or judgment, and to tell them of the eternal glories of the next life. Then what of biblical judgment? When most NDErs claim that they have a new desire to help others, in what *direction* do they seek to help? It often does not seem to be along biblical lines. And to what extent does their greater compassion and empathy extend into theological universalism and syncretism? If they are more tolerant, aren't they more tolerant of all religions? Don't NDEs often teach people that "all pathways lead to God" (1:149)?

If NDErs love more, how do they do it? And what are the implications of an impersonal, unconditional love bereft of moral absolutes? Do NDErs have an unconditional love for the biblical Jesus and Christian doctrines? And where's the care in accepting others just as they are without the desire to share the gospel and promote biblical living?

It should be obvious that the "positive changes" reported by NDErs need qualification. By and large, these changes are often positive in a humanistic or occult sense, but not a biblical sense—and that makes all the difference in the world. If the NDE has been an occult experience, then all of these categories are going to be influenced by the nature of that experience. What this means is that the *aftereffects* of the NDE conform to the *experience* of the NDE. Truly positive NDEs bear good fruit (see Question 7). NDEs that initially seem positive but aren't, do not bear good fruit. As Jesus declared, "a bad tree cannot bear good fruit" (Matthew 7:18 NIV). If the NDE is frequently occult and demonic (14:10-27), then its real fruit is not going to be good—regardless of surface appearances.

In *Deceived by the Light*, Dr. Groothuis discusses the lack of holiness that is a characteristic feature of reported NDEs. Many NDErs seem to come back entirely unconcerned with the biblical category of sin, because sins are supposedly viewed differently in the next life and hardly seem consequential at all (14:15). "Such a perspective dulls or eliminates the sting of sin and evil, and embraces the kind of Pollyanna theology that excludes real tragedy. In a tear-stained world shocked and saddened by desperate refugees, bloody tribalism, rape, child abuse, abortion-on-demand, drug addiction, and all manner of ills, there is good reason to question such postmortem 'wisdom'" (15:96).

Betty Eadie's *Embraced by the Light* illustrates the lack of concern with God's holiness. According to Eadie, a member of the antiChristian Mormon religion (41), even "Jesus" Himself, who guided her NDE, would never "do or say anything that would offend me" (20:72). But when God can never offend sinners, we are all in trouble.

In no NDE study we are aware of has the positive category of "loving God" in a biblical sense ever been included. Where is the biblical holiness in the reported NDEs? Where is the worship of the biblical Jesus? Where is the biblical sense of guilt? Where is the command to love and obey the biblical God? Where is the biblical teaching on eternal punishment? Where is the revelation of God's character as it is revealed scripturally? If these are absent from the NDE, then it seems the NDE is anything but heavenly. In that these experiences are frequently reported as being "spiritual" (vs. "religious"), all this makes sense: God is impersonal love and energy; there are sensations of pantheism; there are no moral absolutes nor is there a final judgment. In light of this, it shouldn't be expected that the categories of "positive change" would be defined in a Christian sense.

Atwater reports what other researchers have noted, that NDErs also become oriented toward the present, away from past and future, because "almost every single person returns knowing time does not exist" (1:82). In his own study, Melvin Morse, M.D., reports, "All of the people in the Transformations study...have experienced the same changes as a result of their NDEs....They are virtually fearless about death. *And* for that matter, virtually fearless about life. They live very firmly 'in the now,' savoring life as it happens, making as much of it as they can" (4:81). "This kind of intense concentration and awareness of the present moment is akin to a person high on marijuana. It is also very similar to the curiosity of a child or someone less educated, as well as to that of other drug users and the mentally ill. All these types of people have little or no concept of past or future. Needs are immediate....For them, there is only now, right now" (1:81).

Of course, if the NDE conveys the idea that time is irrelevant and that this timelessness removes one from the "tyranny of time," and if the NDE induces a kind of existentialist "living for the moment" perspective, it is not surprising people might find difficulty with their new lives. This finding has many moral and spiritual ramifications.

In conclusion, a closer look at the research to date reveals that many NDEs are anything but heavenly.

Section II
Related Issues

7. *What are some problems of near-death research? Are there spiritually profitable and godly NDEs?*

If one examines the major books and research conducted into NDEs, one discovers that most NDE researchers generally seem to have a basic "New Age" interest, background, or philosophy. Cherie Sutherland, whose Ph.D. dissertation was popularized for *Reborn in the Light*, speaks of her mystical experiences and daily practice of yoga (3:xix-vi). Raymond Moody and Elisabeth Kubler-Ross, the two dominant figures in the field, are both spiritists (14:26/28:68-71). P.M.H. Atwater writes, "Long before my near-death experiences occurred, I had reached professional status in the field of psychicism and the pursuit of metaphysical knowledge. My particular expertise at that time centered around the areas of: meditation, hypnotherapy, astrology, numerology, colorology, trance mediumship, dehaunting houses, out-of-body traveling, and sensitivity training" (1:137). Richard Kohr is a member of the research committee for the Edgar Cayce instituted ARE, a group specializing in psychic investigation and practice (29:152). Kenneth Ring's New Age preferences are evident in his books and articles. Karlis Osis,

D. Scott Rogo, Frederick Myers, Jean-Baptist Delacour, and many others are or were either parapsychologists, psychic researchers, or occultists (14:14/28:66,77).

The dominance of researchers with a New Age or mystical bias in the NDE field underscores the importance of assessing the relevance of their interpretations. To what extent are their research findings colored by their presuppositions? Is important data being ignored because of a desire to confirm personal worldviews?

The comments of one of the most respected researchers, Dr. Michael Sabom, are also relevant,

> It is my belief that much confusion exists about the spiritual, and specifically Christian, interpretation of the near-death experience. Some of this confusion is a result of the relative lack of Christian *researchers* doing primary research—that is data collection and analysis of NDE's....Non-Christians, on the other hand, have prolifically published work on the NDE and have jumped on this experience as confirming their own *a priori* New Age and Universalist assumptions....Unfortunately, NDE research and interpretation is easily influenced by the world view of the researcher, and this in turn affects the emphasis and "spin" placed on the results. My current work aims at beginning to look at the NDE from a *Christian researcher's* standpoint....Here I examined the content and effect of the NDE in the lives of conservative, liberal and non-Christians.... Does the NDE truly draw people away from organized religion?...Does the NDE affect the "intrinsic religiosity" (as measured by an objective scale with published validity) of Christians and non-Christians alike? Does the NDE affect the prayer lives of Christians and non-Christians in a similar fashion? Who has pleasant (i.e. "heavenly") and unpleasant (i.e. "hellish") NDE's? Are Christian NDErs imbued with the same "psychic powers" that non-Christian NDErs have been reported to possess? How does the NDE affect the marriages and beliefs in reincarnation of Christian experiencers? Most importantly, how do these results fit with biblical truth? (See 30:2.)

As Christian research begins, it will be interesting to see to what extent researcher bias has colored modern public perception of the NDE. We should remember that it is easy for non-Christians to misunderstand true Christianity.

Researchers could easily classify Mormons as true Christians or Jehovah's Witnesses as Christian fundamentalists. This would skew their interpretation of "Christian" NDEs and their aftereffects in the lives of "Christians."

Obviously, only the NDEs of true Christians can offer valid insights into the Christian NDE. In contrast to the findings of most NDE researchers dominated by a New Age perspective, the 1982 research of Sabom suggested NDEs strengthened religious beliefs, although, in the following examples, this seems to have occurred primarily among uncommitted or "worldly" Christians:

> The religious views of persons encountering an NDE were commonly strengthened by the experience itself. This strengthening of previous beliefs was usually evidenced by a marked increase in formal religious activity or personal commitment. One man put it this way:...
>
> "It's brought me closer to the Lord, also, and the Bible. And I try to go along with both of them and those guidelines....I used to go out and get wild and get drunk. But not anymore....I was not only hurting me but my wife and kids. I realized that from these experiences [NDEs] I care more than I did...and it's brought my family closer."...
>
> A vivid transcendental NDE enriched the religious faith of yet another man, who now confessed that he was 100 percent committed to the Lord: "This [experience] has taken a lot of the load off me. But I still have struggles in living the faith, but I realize the grace of God takes care of all that....The Lord has allowed me through this experience to separate what is important from what is not important. That has been a terrific boon to me....He made me through this experience to be able to completely put myself in the hands of the Lord and totally believe....You can imagine what a boon that is to my life to be able to totally commit myself 100 percent without any reservation" (8:129-31).

Dr. Nina Helene conducted the first in-depth, exploratory, structured interview study of biblical near-death experiences (BNDEs) with 40 subjects:

> Before their BNDE many individuals experienced a deep dissatisfaction with their lives, their spiritual experience and their faith. After their BNDE they

either turned to God and Christ for the first time or returned to Him. Afterwards, they desired a deep faith and more real experience of Christ which would change them....The emotional and spiritual stability of their lives following their BNDEs contrasted dramatically to the broken, spiritually nomadic lives of NDErs who encountered beings of light....The BNDE is distinctive for individuals with varying Christian beliefs, even for those with no religious beliefs, who were being prayed for in the name of Jesus Christ before or during their BNDEs. This praying was unknown to most experiencers at the time of their NDEs....Sixty-three percent of the accounts contained detailed biblical content...(Letter of February 2, 1996).

Another Christian researcher, using 22 conservative Christians, 13 liberal Christians, and 12 non-Christians found no basic difference between NDEs among Christians and non-Christians. [Note that Christian research on this subject may have at least two different approaches: 1) Positive or "biblical" NDEs (that have a positive, biblical impact—whether or not the person is a Christian at the point of occurrence), and 2) examining NDEs among both Christians and non-Christians.]

Apparently one's experience in an NDE has something to do with one's views prior to the NDE. In one case, New Age occult beliefs could become powerfully confirmed; in another, agnostic or nominally Christian beliefs could absorb the "teachings" of the experience, whatever they happen to be. In yet another case, a person could be converted to Christian faith (e.g., 8:130).

Christian NDE research would need to take into account factors relative to outcome such as spiritual history and current degree of spiritual commitment (for Christians) and prior interest in the occult (or occult involvement in one's family history) (for non-Christians), since such things could open the door to spiritual deception in the NDE, potentially even for Christians (31). The specific NDE content (especially messages) and the implications, doctrinal or otherwise; the short- and long-term results of the NDE and the problem of properly interpreting one's perceptions in an ineffable experience one has no control over are also relevant issues.

Some firsthand, preliminary, small sample research by evangelicals is beginning in this area, but it will be some time before firm conclusions relating to how NDEs differ among Christian and non-Christians can be scientifically documented. When hundreds of cases of Christian NDEs are on file and carefully evaluated, then and only then may reliable conclusions be drawn.

We believe that long-term, carefully controlled research concerning genuine Christian and non-Christian NDEs will reveal important differences. If no differences in NDEs exist between Christians, non-Christians, New Agers, etc., the implications are not small. For example, when angels appear to Christians, what if they act no differently than the impersonating spirits (demons) who appear as "angels" to non-Christians or New Agers? Have the *unsaved* dead ever made appearances to Christians and given messages? (Biblically this seems hardly credible—see Luke 16:26 and 2 Peter 2:9.) Does God permit the saved dead to appear to Christians in NDEs to deliver messages? If so, are the messages consistent with biblical revelation? Do Christians develop psychic powers from NDEs? For a number of reasons this is problematic and would require thorough evaluation. For example, did such persons have psychic powers prior to both their conversion and their NDE?

Regardless, while we must be careful to recognize the presence of clear occult influences in the NDE phenomenon (14), we should *not* conclude that all NDEs are necessarily evil or deceptive. God can use NDEs in the lives of anyone He chooses. The experience itself (the information it conveys) and the results of the experience are part of what determines its source. NDEs can be occult, Christian, or neutral, the latter having no discernible occult or anti-Christian elements.

J. Isamu Yamamoto recounts the story of "Dan," a "very active" homosexual who contracted gonorrhea. A treatment option was given of either ten days of antibiotics or a single massive dose by injection. He chose the latter, which caused him to go into anaphylactic shock. Dan had a rather "typical" NDE where he met a brilliant light—but he knew that the source of the light was Jesus Christ. He heard a voice come from the light that said, "It is not time to come into My Father's kingdom. You have not lived as I intended. Go back and glorify Me."

Dan awoke at that moment, back in his body, a committed believer in Jesus Christ. He left his homosexual lifestyle and joined a strong and supportive Christian community. To this day, Dan glorifies God for giving him a new chance to live his life in accordance with biblical teaching. Yamamoto "checked the sources behind Dan's story and discovered that his testimony was reliable" (32:22).

The personal experience of cardiologist Maurice Rawlings in resuscitating NDErs who have had a negative experience also indicates that the NDE may lead to conversion and saving faith in Christ (17/33).

Dr. Groothuis cites a similar experience relayed to him by Christian cardiologist Mark Sheenan. As an individual who went into cardiac arrest was being resuscitated, he looked up at the doctor and cried, "I'm not going up there!" He told the doctor, "I saw Jesus standing next to you. But Jesus did not know me or accept me! What do I do!" Dr. Sheenan prayed with the man to repent of his sins and accept Christ as his Lord and Savior, which he did. Although he died shortly after this event, his wife reported her husband was at "peace with the Lord" (15:87).

God is, after all, sovereign and can intervene in a near-death situation anytime He chooses for His own purposes. There are many testimonies on record of former occultists or non-Christians who were in the midst of a particular occult experience or sin when God intervened dramatically in their lives and the result was conversion to Christianity.

8. What can we do to help people who are suffering consequences from their NDEs?

In light of what we have seen, it is clear that many of the NDEs experienced by non-Christians are deceptive and consequential. They are deceptive because, although the experience is associated with death, it gives a false portrait of what death truly involves biblically for the person outside of Christ. They are consequential in that the dramatic personality and world-view changes, the baptism into the occult and development of psychic powers, and the entire complex of post-NDE effects make readjustment to normal life difficult.

So what can we do to help people who have had NDEs? First, if a committed Christian has had an NDE, one should not conclude that their experience was occult or deceptive unless such elements are clearly present. As we saw, God may work through NDEs in the lives of both believers and unbelievers; the contents of the experience itself must determine its spiritual legitimacy. Christians with this experience should seek to determine what God was saying to them personally (if anything). But they should be careful not to read any theological or other conclusion into their experience that is unbiblical or to "fill in" what the Bible is silent upon. For example, claims to have experienced the actual places of heaven or hell must be viewed critically since being in heaven or hell and experiencing heavenly or hellish NDEs are not necessarily the same thing, even if they seem to be. Broadcasting descriptions of what heaven or hell are "really" like would seem unwise since the canon of Scripture is now closed. When the apostle Paul was taken into heaven he "heard inexpressible things, things that man is *not permitted* to tell" (2 Corinthians 12:4 NIV, emphasis added).

How should we respond to non-Christians who have had NDEs? If the experience clearly involved occult elements such as meeting with the dead or receiving unbiblical revelations, we should seek to explain why these experiences were not true to biblical teaching and the consequences of believing them. It is not necessary to deny their experience, only to properly evaluate it and make certain the person understands that, no matter how profound, it does not change what God declares is true— that apart from faith in Christ a person who truly dies will face God in judgment. Any resulting psychic abilities should be renounced, unbiblical revelations in the NDE should be rejected, and all potential future occult involvement avoided.

Certainly, many of the problems of readjustment associated with NDEs can be successfully dealt with if people understand that this experience is not necessarily the positive or glorious one it seems to be. Indeed, in many cases it is better forgotten. If people further understand that their experience was no different from many other pagan, mystical experiences and these also have negative consequences, they may see that their own ability to truly readjust is dependent upon the degree to which they *reject* what was learned in the NDE. This will enable them to not allow their NDE to interfere with the importance of their marriage and family, and their love will not become "impersonal" but will remain practical in word and deed. It is also up to the NDEr to make sure they do not broadcast false and unbiblical views about life and death.

For children who have had NDEs, one should be careful to evaluate the experience judiciously, to not raise problems that do not exist, and to not be overly concerned unless the child is reporting personally drawn conclusions from the NDE that are clearly unbiblical.

9. What will heaven be like?

Many fine books have been written on heaven, and we encourage the reader to read these for greater insight into the eternal existence of the redeemed (34). Due to space considerations, we can only give a brief thumbnail sketch (9). (Looking up the Scriptures cited in this question and the next will be helpful.)

Heaven is not a perpetual vacation—something that would be terribly boring after only 50 years. Heaven is an eternity of purpose and destiny. After the largest conceivable amount of time multiplied indefinitely by the largest conceivable amount of time, eternity has only just begun. Therefore, heaven must not only be beyond our imagination, but commensurate with the nature and demands of a redeemed eternity itself.

Heaven will be an infinitely superb, multi-faceted and glorious paradise because an infinitely superb, multi-faceted, glorious God lives there. Words such as grandeur, exquisite, magnificent, marvelous, resplendent, elegant, and superluxurious are, at best, shadows of descriptions. In fact, we think it will take an eternity of years to explore only part of heaven.

Heaven is a real and substantial place for real and substantial people. In this place, Jesus told us that we would be glorified and exalted with Him. We will reign with Him "forever and ever" (Revelation 20:6; 22:5) and have spiritual bodies (Ephesians 2:6; Romans 8:11-17; Philippians 3:21, 1 John 3:2). We will also judge (and perhaps rule) the angels (1 Corinthians 6:3).

In heaven, everything that makes life here unpleasant or tortuous will be forever vanquished. Those present in heaven will never experience pain, sadness, sorrow, depression, sickness, death, sin, evil, selfishness, fatigue, or suffering of any kind "for the old order of things has passed away" (Revelation 21:4; see also 22:3).

Heaven will be a place of indescribable love, beauty, peace, joy, happiness, rest, adventure, excitement, and union and fellowship with God (Revelation 21:4)—multiplied to the degree suggested by what a infinitely loving, omnipotent, and omniscient God would do in eternity for those He willingly sacrificed His only Son for here. Scripture itself teaches that if God has given us His own Son now, how much more will He give us throughout eternity? (See Romans 8:32; 1 Corinthians 2:9; 3:21-23.)

Life in heaven will be beyond our wildest imagination experientially. If heaven, by definition, is devoid of everything old that is negative it must also be saturated with everything new that is positive: "He who was seated on the throne said, 'I am making everything new!' Then he said, 'Write this down, for these words are trustworthy and true'" (Revelation 21:5). Thus, heaven will be a place of eternal security and protection where God's creation is redeemed and transformed into an absolutely perfect new earth and heavens (cf., Romans 8:18-23; Revelation chapters 21 and 22). In this never-to-be-equaled universe, which could be infinite, we will be able to explore, and never exhaust the ability to explore—just as we will never be able to exhaust our exploration of all there is to know and experience of an infinite God.

Obviously, since we are finite beings—there will be never-ending growth in knowledge, truth and wisdom—of God, the creation, angels, and men and women. We will not only have joyous, intimate, personal fellowship with God, Jesus, and the angels but also with billions of redeemed people who lived throughout history—and with whatever else God may have created. Yet service and worship to God will be one of our *greatest* joys. As suggested by the parable of the talents (Matthew 25:14-29; Luke 19:11-26), we will also enjoy rewards for service given on earth. These will probably include different positions of honor and authority in heaven. However, *all* our heavenly blessings and glories will be eternal and indestructible (1 Peter 1:3,4).

But we must also remember that there is far, far more we *don't* know about heaven than we do know; its beauties and glories are literally inconceivable to us now. We should expect nothing less from a future kingdom prepared by Jesus, Himself, for those He loves and died for (Matthew 25:34; John 14:2). Apart from Christ, there is no such thing as *real* life—now or forever.

First Corinthians 2:9 only hints at what awaits those who have made Jesus their Lord and Savior: "Things which eye has not seen and ear has not heard, and which have not entered the heart of man, all that God has prepared for those who love Him." Indeed, "the sufferings of this present time are not worthy to be compared with the glory that is to be revealed to us" (Romans 8:18). In sum, we will inherit all that God *is* and all that God *has* (1 Corinthians 3:21-23)—

in a true paradise as God originally intended it. And, as a result, "the righteous will shine like the sun in the kingdom of their Father" forever (Matthew 13:43 NIV).

10. What will life in hell be like?

Hell may be ridiculed and outdated in the minds of many people, but that does not change its reality. Given the infinite holiness of God, one thing is certain—the strongest arguments against hell will be silenced forever on the other side. (Polls since 1944 indicate that although 50 to 60 percent of people believe in hell, only 3 to 4 percent think their chances are good of going there (14:10). Many people may think they will never go to hell because they don't "deserve" it. But unless they repent and turn to Jesus for forgiveness of sins, that will be their fate.

The single most authoritative person in human history, Jesus Christ, spoke often of the reality of an eternal hell (for example, see Matthew 25:41,46). He warned, "wide is the gate and broad is the road that leads to destruction, and many enter through it," while "only a few" find eternal life in heaven (Matthew 7:13,14). Jesus also said, "If you do not believe that I am the one I claim to be, you will indeed die in your sins" (John 8:24 NIV), and He asked, "For what will a man be profited if he gains the whole world, and forfeits his soul?" (Matthew 16:26).

The most predominant feature of hell will be the eternal absence of an infinitely loving God and the never-ending presence of just punishment for individual sins (2 Thessalonians 1:9; Daniel 12:2; Matthew 10:28). Hell involves degrees of punishment according to the works done in this life (Matthew 11:21-24; 23:23; Luke 12:47-48). In contrast to what most people think, those who are condemned to hell will recognize and understand the perfect justice of their presence there. Popular views of universalism (all will be saved), variations on conditional immortality (the unsaved will be annihilated), and ideas of the opportunity for salvation after death are impossible to defend scripturally (10). Because of God's infinite righteousness, hell cannot logically be considered immoral. But it could actually be immoral for God to save everyone irrespective of their will or to annihilate those having intrinsic value, those created in His image (9:169-71).

Hell is a subject that all people should contemplate for many reasons, among them (9:157-80):

1) It is obviously in our own best interest to escape going to hell. Apart from Christ, people will go there, but

this fate can easily be avoided in this life (see John 1:12; 3:16-18; 5:24; 6:47).

2) God does not desire that anyone perish and has done all He can, this side of death, within the limits of His character and the human condition, to save all people (see 2 Peter 3:9; Acts 17:26-31).

It is entirely possible that, given God's infinite knowledge of what every created being would do under every possible circumstance, God has so structured human existence so as to save the greatest number. Further, it is equally credible that "of all the possible persons God could have created, the vast majority of those who would have rejected Christ never get created in the first place. The number of people who reject Christ may [actually] be an act of mercy on God's part" (9:178). It is even possible that, given God's holy character and human responsibility, there is *no* world God could have created in which all created persons would have freely accepted Christ. Apparently, "God prefers a world in which some persons freely reject Christ but the number of saved is maximized over a world in which a few trust Christ and none are lost." Thus, "the actual world contains an optimal balance between saved and unsaved, and those who are unsaved would never have received Christ under any circumstances" (9:180).

3) Hell is not unjust. The one true God who has revealed Himself as *infinitely* loving and merciful has also spoken of the reality of eternal separation from Him; therefore, it cannot be inconsistent with His love, justice, and mercy.

We don't usually balk at the devil going to hell because we assume the devil is bad enough and God just enough to warrant it. Only when it comes to *us*, do we question its justness. But if it is just for the devil, can we assume it is never just for those of us who are "like" the devil in our attitudes and actions—especially as they are directed toward God? (See John 8:44, cf., 1 John 3:8.) Indeed, apart from hell, justice becomes a myth. Even if someone like Adolph Hitler were punished for billions of years and then brought into eternal heaven or annihilated, his punishment, compared to eternity, would be meaningless. All creation will one day understand this (cf., Romans 3:4-6).

4) Hell is not a place where God actively tortures people endlessly as if He were the director of some kind of torture chamber. Hell was made for the devil and his angels (Matthew 25:41), not man. But people who continue

their rebellion against God must suffer the just judgment of their sins. Since God will not permit unrighteousness or anything unholy to enter heaven (Revelation 21:27; Habakkuk 1:13), there must be some other place for the unrighteous to inhabit in eternity. If the unrighteous are not permanently quarantined from the righteous, all we have is an instant and eternal replay of life on earth—and this is surely not heaven! There will be psychological and physical anguish and torment in hell, but this will result primarily from the conditions of hell and people's own choices and realizations, not from God actively inflicting their torment. A judge and jury who justly send a man to prison do not torment him; his own choices and the conditions of prison do.

5) Sin committed against God is not like sin committed against others. Sinning against an infinite being requires an infinite punishment which, for finite creatures, can only be experienced as eternal punishment.

Further, the amount of time it takes to commit a sin has no direct relationship to the punishment it deserves. A bank teller may plan an embezzlement for months while his accomplice may murder someone in a moment. The evil of a crime is related more to the *nature* of the crime and the *one* against whom it is committed than the time it takes to commit it. Everyone knows that a man having sex with a prostitute is not the same as a man having sex with an innocent little girl. No one can accurately gauge how an infinite God, whose holiness is unmeasurable, responds to even the smallest human sin. One would think that, for a literally infinite Being, even the most minute human sin is fully heinous and worthy of eternal punishment.

Also, because the unredeemed *are* unredeemed, they continue to sin *after* death and apparently will continue to sin inwardly *forever* (Matthew 8:12). But the only *just* punishment for eternal sin would seem to be eternal punishment. In light of the above, the bottom line is that a good God cannot be unjust in punishing people eternally. Hell is no more or less than *perfect* justice, as it must be (Romans 3:4-6). And this means there *is* final justice. Indeed, few things in life are as satisfying as justice. Further, hell must also be in full harmony with the love of God: "God loves justice, holiness, and righteousness *so much* that He created hell. The love of God for His own nature, His law, His universe, and His people, makes hell a *product of love* as well as justice" (35:38e).

6) Our choice *for* God is important to Him (see Luke 13:34). People who refuse Christ in this life would be quite unlikely to accept Him in the next life, in hell, because their basic nature is not altered. If Scripture declares the unredeemed are God's enemies who want nothing to do with Him (Acts 4:25-27; Romans 1:18-32; 5:6-10), why would anything change just because someone died? Even if they somehow did decide for Christ, it would only be to escape the punishments of hell rather than to love and obey God. They would not be choosing God and Jesus and, thus would not be suited for eternal life with them in heaven. No one wants to live forever with someone they dislike intensely. The more you understand the nature of heaven as being infused with the nature of God, the more the idea that the unredeemed would not enjoy heaven makes sense. And the longer we refuse God's gift of mercy now, the harder it becomes to accept it later. Every day, in almost every way, we are either moving closer to God or further from Him. At the end of an unrepentant life, God simply grants our wishes.

C.S. Lewis emphasized, "There are only two kinds of people in the end: those who say to God, 'Thy will be done,' and those to whom God says, in the end, '*Thy* will be done'" (36:69). He also said, "If a game is played it must be possible to lose it. If the happiness of a creature lies in self-surrender, no one can make that surrender but himself (though many can help him to make it) and he may refuse. I would pay any price to be able to say truthfully 'all will be saved.' But my reason retorts, 'without their will, or with it?' If I say, 'without their will' I at once perceive a contradiction; how can the supreme voluntary act of self-surrender be involuntary? If I say 'with their will,' my reason replies 'how if they *will not* give in?'" (37:118).

7) God will do what is just in this life and the next. Hebrews 11:6 says that God rewards those who seek Him and Acts 10:35 says, "In every nation the man who fears Him and does what is right, is welcome to Him." Abraham asked, "Shall not the Judge of all the earth do right?" (Genesis 18:25 KJV), and the psalmist said, "He will judge the world with justice and the peoples with unfaltering fairness" (Psalm 98:9 BERKELEY).

Thus, not everyone experiences the same degree of pain in hell since there are degrees of punishment (Luke 12:35-48; Matthew 10:15). Those who were less evil in this life are not punished to the same degree as those who were more evil. God is unable to violate His holy character and give any person more punishment than he deserves. This means that God, who is infinite in knowledge, knows the perfectly righteous and just punishment for every person who has ever lived.

Conclusion

Although "you can't avoid death and taxes," some people manage to avoid taxes. But death is another story; everyone born faces death as an unavoidable certainty. Biblically speaking, people fear death because they intuitively sense judgment after death. In this sense, the fear of death is all to the good. According to Scripture, "the wages of sin is death" (Romans 6:23), and, "It is appointed for men to die once and after this comes judgment" (Hebrews 9:27). According to Romans (chapters 1 and 2), all men not only know a righteous God exists, but they also know that they are sinful. The conclusion is that they know that apart from forgiveness they will face God in judgment. Regardless of the level at which men understand this, the fear of death is something that is intuitive and part of what helps them consider the gospel.

In cultures where a pagan or occult view of death prevails (and death is more accepted than in Western society), the fear of death may be lessened somewhat but the fear remains. Most people who say they don't fear death are speaking on a surface level; were we to see inside their hearts it would be another matter. Thus, in a study of different populations of people in varying degrees of health and illness, "all populations studied have shown the same general pattern of death fear…" (16b:366).

People also intuitively sense they will live forever because, in fact, they will (Ecclesiastes 3:11). What they fear is the abysmal depths of the unknown. The angel of death—a never distant companion—will one day extend its wings. Every individual will then face eternity. The only question is where eternity will be spent. The choice now is as personal as it is monumental.

For those who desire to live forever in heaven, we suggest the following prayer:

> Lord Jesus Christ, I humbly acknowledge that I have sinned in my thinking, speaking, and acting, that I am guilty of deliberate wrongdoing, that my

sins have separated me from Your Holy presence, and that I am helpless to commend myself to You.

I firmly believe that You died on the cross for my sins, bearing them in Your own body, and suffering in my place the condemnation I deserved.

I have thoughtfully counted the cost of following You. I sincerely repent, turning away from my past sins. I am willing to surrender to You as my Lord and Master.

So now I come to You. I believe that You have been patiently standing outside the door knocking for a long time. I now open the door. Come in, Lord Jesus, and be my Savior and my Lord forever. Amen (38:25).

Becoming a Christian involves a serious commitment. New Christians should attend a church where Jesus is honored, read their Bible daily, and offer their prayers and lives to the God who is there and hears them.

Reference Bibliography

Note to Reader: Footnotes in the text are keyed to this bibliography. For example, 3:10 refers to reference number 3, page 10. A small "e" (after the reference means emphasis has been added.

1. P.M.H. Atwater, *Coming Back to Life: The Aftereffects of the Near-death Experience*, New York: Dodd Mead & Co., 1988.
2. Raymond A. Moody, Jr., *The Light Beyond*, New York: Bantam, 1989.
3. Cherie Sutherland, *Reborn in the Light: Life After Near-death Experiences*, New York: Bantam, 1995.
4. Melvin Morse with Paul Perry, *Transformed by the Light: The Powerful Effect of Near-death Experiences on People's Lives*, New York: Ballentine/Ivy Books, 1994.
5. Kenneth Ring, *Heading Toward Omega: In Search of the Meaning of the Near-Death Experience*, New York: William Morrow, 1985.
6. Joel Martin and Patricia Romanowski, *We Don't Die: George Anderson's Conversations with the Other Side*, New York: Berkley Books, 1989.
7. Raymond Moody with Paul Perry, *Reunions: Visionary Encounters with Departed Loved Ones*, New York: Villard Books, 1993.
8. Michael B. Sabom, *Recollections of Death: A Medical Investigation*, New York: Harper & Row, 1982.

9. Gary R. Habermas and J.P. Moreland, *Immortality: the Other Side of Death*, Nashville: Thomas Nelson Publishers, 1992.

10. For detailed refutation, see Robert A. Morey, *Death and the Afterlife*, Minneapolis: Bethany House Publishers, 1984.

11. Elizabeth L. Hillstrom, *Testing the Spirits*, Downer's Grove, IL: InterVarsity, 1995.

12. Robert Basil, ed., *Not Necessarily the New Age: Critical Essays*, New York: Prometheus, 1988; John Snyder, *Reincarnation Versus Resurrection*, Chicago: Moody Press, 1984; Norman Geisler and J. Yutaka Amano, *The Reincarnation Sensation*, Wheaton, IL: Tyndale House, 1987.

13. John Ankerberg and John Weldon, *The Facts on UFOs and Other Supernatural Phenomena* and *The Facts on Spirit Guides,* Eugene, OR: Harvest House Publishers, 1992.

14. John Ankerberg and John Weldon, *The Facts on Life After Death*, Eugene, OR: Harvest House Publishers, 1992.

15. Doug Groothuis, *Deceived by the Light*, Eugene, OR: Harvest House Publishers, 1995.

16. Cf., Robert L. Menz, "The Denial of Death and the Out-of-the-Body Experience," *Journal of Religion and Health*, Winter 1984; M. A. Rigdon, "Levels of Death Fear: A Factor Analysis," *Death Education*, vol. 6, 1983.

17. Maurice Rawlings, *To Hell and Back: Life After Death, Startling New Evidence*, Nashville: Thomas Nelson Publishers,1993.

18. P.M.H. Atwater, *Beyond the Light: What Isn't Being Said About Near Death Experience*, New York: Birch Lane Press, 1994.

19. Melvin Morse, *Closer to the Light: Learning from the Near-death Experiences of Children*, New York: Villard Books, 1990.

20. Betty J. Eadie with Curtis Taylor, *Embraced by the Light*, New York: Bantam, 1994.

21. Pat Rodegast, *Emmanuel's Book*, Weston, CT: Friends Press, 1986.

22. Joel Martin and Patricia Romanowski, *Our Children Live Forever: George Anderson's Messages from Children on the Other Side*, New York: Berkley Books, 1994.

23. Dannion Brinkley with Paul Perry, *Saved by the Light*, New York: Harper Paperbacks, 1995.

24. Kenneth Ring, *The Omega Project: Near-death Experiences, UFO Encounters, and Mind at Large*, New York: Quill, 1992.

25. John Weldon, Zola Levitt, *Psychic Healing: An Exposé of an Occult Phenomenon*, Dallas: Zola Levitt Ministries, 1991.

26. See ref. 14, pp. 70-71, citing Brooks Alexander and Mark Albrecht, "Thanatology, Death and Dying," *Spiritual Counterfeits Project Journal*, April 1977.

27. Lennie Kronish, "Elisabeth Kubler-Ross: Messenger of Love," *Yoga Journal*, September-October 1976, pp. 18-20; K. Coleman,

"Elisabeth Kubler-Ross in the Afterworld of Entities," *New West,* July 30, 1979.

28. John Weldon, Zola Levitt, *Is There Life After Death?* Dallas: Zola Levitt Ministries, 1991.

29. Richard Kohr, "Near-death Experiences, Altered States, Psi-sensitivity," *Anabiosis*, vol. 3, no. 2 (December 1983).

30. Letter to John Weldon, October 28, 1995.

31. Cf., the writings of Kurt Koch, Merril Unger, and C. Fred Dickason as they relate to a critique of the occult and its influence upon Christians and non-Christians.

32. J. Isamu Yamamoto, "The Near Death Experience, Part 1," *Christian Research Journal*, Spring 1992.

33. Maurice Rawlings, *Beyond Death's Door*, Nashville: Thomas Nelson Publishers, 1978.

34. Esp. John Gilmore, *Probing Heaven: Key Questions on the Hereafter*, Grand Rapids, MI: Baker Book House, 1989, and Joni Eareckson Tada, *Heaven Your Real Home*, Grand Rapids, MI: Zondervan, 1995.

35. Robert A. Morey, *Introduction to Defending the Faith*, Southbridge, MA: Crowne Publications, 1989.

36. C.S. Lewis, *The Great Divorce*, New York: MacMillan, 1946.

37. C.S. Lewis, *The Problem of Pain*, New York: MacMillan, 1971.

38. Taken from John Stott, *Becoming a Christian*, Downer's Grove, IL: InterVarsity, 1950.

39. Kenneth Ring, referring to Raymond Moody's, *Life After Life*, foreword, in ref. 3.

40. Ernest Becker, *The Denial of Death*, New York: The Free Press, 1973.

41. John Ankerberg and John Weldon, *Behind the Mask of Mormonism*, Eugene, OR: Harvest House Publishers, 1996.

42. Kenneth Ring, "From Alpha to Omega: Ancient Mysteries and the Near Death Experience," *Anabiosis*, vol. 5, no. 2 (1986).

43. Richard Abanes, Paul Carden, "A Special Report: What is Betty Eadie Hiding?" *Christian Research Journal*, Winter 1994.